Walking On Water

A Faith Walk

Copyright

AC Creative products are available in bulk quantity for sales, fundraising and educational purposes. For details, contact AC Creative at www.IWRITEITNOW.COM

Walking On Water *A Faith Walk*
By Ericka Wilson
Published by AC Creative
1440 W. Taylor #835
Chicago, IL 60607
iwin@writenow.global

Dedication

To my son Kahlil Knox who has been with me through the good and bad times of my life. You didn't once complain even though we moved every year from state to state, city to town, from apartments to houses, from shelters to living in our car. You did not have a "normal" childhood. Yet, as I was learning to trust and walk in the supernatural with Jesus you were with me every step of the way. Not that you had a choice! I would do it all over again with no regrets. Why? Because the experiences we had has made you the most amazingly strong and caring young man in the Lord that I know. You have been the one constant person in my life besides Jesus and I wouldn't trade what we've been through together with Him for anything.

Special Thanks

First and foremost, I give glory and honor to my Father God and my Lord Jesus to whom without Him I am nothing. He is so faithful even when we are not.

To William Moore to whom without his help over the years I would not be where I am today. Thank you for allowing the Lord to use you. I pray for you to be at peace and that you will find your purpose partner.

To Georgianne and Ernie for your generosity of giving us timeshare in Hawaii.

To Deborah, Cynthia, and Barbara what would I do without your prayers. Thank you from the bottom of my heart for your constant prayers for me and my family during this time.

Last, but not least to my other heart, my oldest son Kristian and my daughter Katherine. Thank you for always supporting and loving me. It is such a joy to see how far Daddy has brought you from and where you are now. Kristian I am so proud of the man of God that you have become. TO GOD BE THE GLORY!!!!

Table of Contents

One day while listening to the radio I heard

true story of faith about a young woman who

God told to go to another country. The young

lady didn't hesitate to obey the call of God, she

just packed her bags and left. She went to the

airport and asked if there was a ticket reserved

for her. She had no money, but that didn't stop

her from doing what the Lord had told her to

do.

It turns out that there was a ticket waiting for

her at the airline counter that she approached.

She got on a plane, flew to the country the Lord told her to go to. While in this country, God used her to preach the gospel, cast out demons, heal the sick and raise the dead. When her work was finished, she left and came home.

I remember hearing this story and thinking, "Wow! Lord, what great faith this young lady possessed.

I would hope that if You were to tell me to do something like that, that I would just up and go without any questions and just obey You.

Then I thought to myself, "Well, I don't know if I could really do that? I don't know if I have that much faith."

Little did I know, I would soon find out how much faith I had.

This story begins in 2010 in Kiefer, Oklahoma.

Walking On Water

A Faith Walk

By Ericka Wilson

A family we knew needed help. We had an extra room so my husband and I opened our home to them. We enjoyed each other and spent a lot of time together worshiping the Lord.

One day, while we were praying for each other the wife prophesied. She gave us this word from the Lord, "When you all move to Georgia the Lord said that you all are to take two trips: one to Florida and one to Hawaii."

I took what was said to heart and I remembered these things. She mentioned

Georgia because, she knew we were in the process of moving to Georgia.

We didn't know where in Georgia, or how long we were going to be in Georgia, we just knew we were to go.

Did we know anyone in Georgia? Yes! At the time I had a spiritual mother and father in Stone Mountain, Georgia. Yet, I knew that we weren't to live in Stone Mountain, Georgia.

I knew this because during my seeking the Lord's face as to where we were to live in

Georgia I kept receiving the song, "Home, Home on the Range," in my heart.

So, I said, "OK, Lord. Either You are going to give us a lot of land, or You are moving us to the country." It turned out He moved us to the country, but not right away.

We left in April, my son was going into his sophomore year in high school. My husband quit his job.

I gave away everything not knowing how long we would be in Georgia or where we would be living. When we left town, we headed toward Stone Mountain, Georgia.

A couple of months after being in Stone Mountain, Georgia the Lord settled us in a little town by the name of Trion, Georgia. It was definitely the country.

We lived at the bottom of a mountain where there were, farms, chickens, dogs, deer, goats and horses.

The Lord had told me while we were in Stone Mountain, Georgia that I would love living in the mountains.

As usual, He was right. It was quiet, serene. There was plenty of space. At night you could clearly see the stars. There were no street lights. The road was mainly gravel. It was peaceful. I took long walks and spent time with the Lord just talking to Him. I found quiet spots alone to just be with Him.

Down the way, there was a neighbor's farm. He had a chapel of on his land. He was kind enough to allow me to pray and praise the Lord in his chapel anytime I wanted. We became very good friends with this neighbor.

At the time we left, we didn't understand why the Lord was moving us to Georgia.

One thing we always knew is that when the Lord moves us there are people that need to be saved, so we just go! As I said before, we didn't know how long we were to be in Georgia.

In June, the Lord settled us in a doublewide four-bedroom trailer on the mountains. I had never lived in a trailer before but, it was a nice one. So, I didn't mind.

Not long afterwards we took our trip to Florida. When it was told us that we were to take two trips: one to Florida and one to Hawaii. I said to myself, "Ok, Florida is easy."

My spiritual mother had given us time share and we could afford it.

When she said that we were to go to Hawaii I said, "Well Lord, that one's on You! You're going to have to make ways out of no ways because we don't have the money for Hawaii.

Not long after we took the trip to Florida my spiritual mother offered us more time share. She said she had plenty and wanted to give us more. As soon as she told me this, my spirit leaped and I knew that it was God making a way for us to go to Hawaii.

Then she asked where we would go? I said, "Hawaii" because, I knew that was where we were to go.

Once, I told her Hawaii she didn't ask me where in Hawaii at first. That was a good thing because the Lord didn't tell me a specific place He just said, "Hawaii."

In September she brought up the subject of giving us time share again. She said that it had to be used by the end of November.

This time she asked me, "Where in Hawaii do you all wanted to go? I said, "You know I don't know where in Hawaii because the Lord just said, "Hawaii." He didn't tell us where. I guess I'll have to ask Him."

As soon as, I said this, the Lord spoke to me. He said, "Maui." My son, who was in the room at the time said, "Maui!" right after I heard the Lord say it in my heart and before I could tell my spiritual mother.

So, I knew when my son said it that it was a confirmation that we were to go to Maui. Now we knew where we were going, we just didn't know when we were going.

When dealing with time share you need to make reservations to see if there are rooms available. Maui is a popular place. We didn't know if they had availability during the time we wanted to go.

We also didn't have an exact date that we wanted to go. We only had and expiration date of November 30th.

I called to see if I could set a date for our trip and there was no availability. The agent said that there were no openings.

I said, "Ok." I knew that the Lord wanted us to go so I just continued to call periodically to see if they had any openings.

We only had three months to choose from and I still didn't know when He wanted us to go.

Therefore, I said, "Well Lord, I guess You will open the door for the month and day You want us to go."

My job is just to believe that God could do the impossible which, I already knew He could do. I continued to call week after week to see if there was any availability in Maui.

One day I called and was told that there was an available date in October. It was the second week in October. I asked the agent if he could hold the reservation for me. The agent replied, "Yes." I needed $158.00 to book the room reservation. At the time I didn't have $158.00.

I asked the agent, "How long can you hold the reservation?" He replied, "We can only hold it for twenty-four hours."

I said, "Ok." So, every twenty-four hours I called

them and asked them to hold the reservation.

 I did this for a couple of weeks until I received

$158.00 which, I had to believe the Lord to

give me.

When I received the money I called back to

confirm the reservation. On the day I did this

the agent told me that the reservation was not

held.

I was disappointed, almost angry.

Then I realized, "Lord, all of this is in Your

hands. I guess that wasn't the day we were to

go. Lord, You know when we are to be there so fix it."

The agent told me that the first date was not available. He then gave me a date a week earlier that was available. I said, "I'll take it!"

It was October 1st. So, I was able to book a resort reservation.

Now we were on our way. We had a room reservation! Or were we on our way?

Now the hard part! We had a place to stay in Maui, but we didn't know how we were getting to Maui. We had no money for three airline tickets to Maui.

I turned to the Lord and said, "Ok Lord! Now we have a place to stay. How are we getting there?"

He brought to mind a young man whom I met before I left Oklahoma. I was introduced to him by another sister in Christ.

This young man worked for the airlines and was known for helping ministers and ministries to fly different places to preach the gospel. It came to me to call him and I did.

I called him and the first thing he said was, "It is a little late in the year. Everyone that I know who may have a ticket to give you have probably used all their tickets." I asked him to please keep checking and looking for someone who may have tickets that they could give us and to get back to me. He agreed.

In the meantime, I prayed. I said, "Lord, You are the one sending us on this trip Thank You for providing. If this is the way, we are to go thank you that he is going to find someone who has some tickets they can give us."

Working for the airlines myself years ago I understand how this works. A ticket from the airlines would be standby but we still wouldn't have to pay as much as we would if we had to pay regular fare.

I still didn't know if he came up with the tickets how we were getting the money to pay for the tickets, but I didn't worry about that.

The Holy Spirit continually encouraged me. He kept songs on my heart about having the victory and being an overcomer.

I stayed in touch with the young man because we didn't have much time before we had to leave.

I believe from the time I made the reservation we were to leave a week later.

I called him several times. When I finally got in touch he told me that he couldn't find anyone who could give me tickets.

Before I called him the Lord put the song, "O'er for Grace to Trust You More. "He kept this song on my heart even after the young man said he couldn't find anyone.

I said, "Ok Lord. This is all You and I trust You."

The Lord also told me that He was sending us because someone needed to be saved. I could have figured that out because everywhere He sends us He does it because someone needs to be saved.

This made me realize the importance of getting to Hawaii.

Walking by faith, I began to buy us clothes for the trip. I began packing. I did everything I could on my end to prepare for this trip.

The devil did everything he could to try to discourage me.

It didn't work. He had my son say that he didn't want to go, he wanted to stay because of football. He had my husband go through something. I got to the point where I told them that this was a family trip and we were all going!

Then I told them, "You know, the Lord has someone He wants to save. If you all don't go, I'll go by myself!" I was determined to go to Hawaii and do what the Lord told me to do.

I had even made arrangements with a sister in Christ to keep my car for seven days.

It was coming down to the wire. It was almost time for us to leave.

I tried to get in touch with the sister who I was going to leave my car with to give her instructions, but I wasn't able to contact her.

Finally, one day I saw her. I said, "Hey Sis, I've been trying to get in touch with you. She then said. "Are you all still going to Hawaii?" I told her, "Yes."

I told her what day but I didn't tell her what time we would be leaving because I didn't know how we were getting on a plane or what time any of the flights were leaving to go to Hawaii.

I told her that I would call her the day before we left to let her know the time we would be leaving.

When that time came I couldn't reach her so we had to obtain parking in the airport parking lot for seven days.

A Faith Walk
DAY 1

It's time to go to Hawaii! The Lord woke me with the song, "We are the Champions," on my heart.

During my daily devotion this morning He gave me the scriptures Revelation 7:9-17 letting me know that He has given us the victory and will deliver us.

Revelation 7:9-17 NIV:

⁹ After this I looked, and there before me was a great multitude that no one could count, from every nation, tribe, people and language, standing before the throne and before the Lamb. They were wearing white robes and were holding palm branches in their hands. ¹⁰ And they cried out in a loud voice:

"Salvation belongs to our God,

who sits on the throne,

and to the Lamb."

¹¹ All the angels were standing around the throne and around the elders and the four living creatures. They fell down on their faces before the throne and worshiped God, ¹² saying:

"Amen!

Praise and glory

and wisdom and thanks and honor

and power and strength

be to our God for ever and ever.

Amen!"

¹³ Then one of the elders asked me, "These in white robes—who are they, and where did they come from?"

¹⁴ I answered, "Sir, you know."

And he said, "These are they who have come out of the great tribulation; they have washed their robes and made them white in the blood

of the Lamb. ¹⁵ *Therefore,*

"they are before the throne of God

> *and serve him day and night in his temple;*

and he who sits on the throne

> *will shelter them with his presence.*

¹⁶ *'Never again will they hunger;*

> *never again will they thirst.*

The sun will not beat down on them,

> *nor any scorching heat.*

¹⁷ *For the Lamb at the center of the throne*

> *will be their shepherd;*

'he will lead them to springs of living water.

> *'And God will wipe away every tear from*

their eyes. '[c] "

We headed for the airport. Not knowing what time, the flights left to go to Hawaii or what airline we would be on.

We left home at 4 a.m. and arrived at the airport at around 6 a.m. We all left in faith believing we were going to get on a plane, trusting the Lord.

Before leaving the Lord put songs on my heart. One was about binding and loosing keys to the Kingdom. The other song was about God supplying our every need.

On the way to the airport I put in the CD that had these songs on it.

We arrived at the airport and parked the car. We didn't know what airline we were to travel on.

 So, I decided that I would approach every ticket counter to see if any of them were holding reservations for us.

No airline was holding a reservation for us. After this, we went and sat down in the American Airlines waiting area.

Then, I went to every airline ticket counter to see what times their flights left and what time they went to Maui.

Waiting, my husband William and I talked to several people about Jesus.

We weren't discouraged even though we didn't know how God was going to do what He told us to do. We were encouraged.
The Holy Spirit kept me encouraged with the words "It Shall Be Done. It Shall Be Done." These words were from the "Binding and Loosing" song from the CD.
He kept these words constantly on my heart. Therefore, I knew what the Lord told me shall

be done. That we shall get on a plane! That we shall go to Hawaii!

Around ten in the morning I said, "Ok everyone, we need to pray because we don't have a ticket and we don't know how we are even getting on a plane. We need to hear from God. "

So we prayed, asking God for wisdom, direction, and for a miracle. After praying we went our separate ways continuing to pray in the Spirit.

As I was praying in the Spirit the Lord said to me, "You have something to bargain with." I replied, "I do?" "He said, "Yes, you have something to bargain with. You have your timeshare." "I said, "Yes, I do have my timeshare."

"He said, Call the man back and tell him that if he finds someone who will give you three tickets to Maui that you will offer that person timeshare that they can be use next year to go anywhere they want to go." I said, "Ok Lord."

I called the man back and said, "If you can find someone who can give us three tickets to Maui, I will give them timeshare to go anywhere they want to go next year."

I then had to explain to him what timeshare was and how it worked. After doing this, he said, "I'll call you back." When I hung up the phone the Lord put the words, "It Shall Be Done, It Shall Be Done," on my heart again. I knew that the man was going to call me back and have tickets for us. Ten minutes later that is exactly what happened.

He called back and said, "I found someone who is willing to give you three standby tickets to Maui." We rejoiced!!! Now, we were on our way! Now we had tickets to get to Maui.

The next flight was about to leave from Atlanta. We were trying to hurry to give the man our information so that he can make a reservation for us.

He also had to give us our routing information. By the time we finished with this the plane had left. We had to wait for the next fight.

Our itinerary was: Atlanta to Dallas, Texas. Dallas, Texas to Los Angeles, California. Los Angeles, California to Maui.

We checked in for the next flight out. All the flights on our trip were open and clear except the flight from Los Angeles, California to Maui.

We were told that we had missed the last flight out of Los Angeles, California and would have to travel the next day from Los Angeles, California to Maui.

We were also told that there were only two flights leaving from Los Angeles, California to Maui and that they were both oversold flights.

This meant that we would have to stay overnight in Los Angeles, California. We had two hundred dollars to our name.

It was a long day. We traveled from Atlanta, Georgia to Dallas, Texas.

When we arrived in Dallas, Texas I wanted to stay overnight there because I knew someone we could stay with. Yet, I was encouraged by the Holy Spirit to continue on to Los Angeles,

California. The Lord reminded me that this was a faith walk."

Every time He reminded me of this I would say, "I know this is a faith walk Lord. Never in my life have I gone to the airport without tickets to get on a plane. So I know this is a faith walk."

We arrived in Los Angeles, California. There was a big time difference and we were tired. We needed a place to stay that was close to the airport and had a shuttle.

I didn't bring my laptop and I wish I had. I called a sister in Christ and asked her to look up cheap hotels for us, there weren't any.

We ended up staying at the same hotel as the crew. It cost one hundred dollars a night. I said to the Lord. "Lord, we only have two hundred dollars for seven days." All He said to me was, "My grace is sufficient."
For the first time after hearing that and this time hearing it from the Lord, I realized that I didn't know what it meant.

I said to the Lord, "Lord, exactly what does that mean anyway? Your grace is sufficient." I didn't receive an answer.

I just kept saying, "Your grace is sufficient." I never received an answer. I guess He said, "She'll figure it out." We got on the shuttle and went to the hotel only to go to bed because, we were exhausted. We had to get up early and catch a 6 a.m. flight.

A Faith Walk
DAY 2

The next morning while in the restroom I spent time with the Lord reading the bible and praying. I asked Him if He could please put us on the first flight out because we had already missed a day of our trip in Maui.

I bound and loosed things. I declared and decreed that we would be on the first plane. During my daily reading the Lord gave me the scripture Matthew 5:17-20.

> *¹⁷ "Do not think that I have come to abolish the Law or the Prophets; I have not come to abolish them but to fulfill them. ¹⁸ For truly I tell you, until heaven and earth disappear, not the smallest letter, not the least stroke of a pen, will by any means disappear from the Law until*

everything is accomplished. ¹⁹ Therefore anyone who sets aside one of the least of these commands and teaches others accordingly will be called least in the kingdom of heaven, but whoever practices and teaches these commands will be called great in the kingdom of heaven. ²⁰ For I tell you that unless your righteousness surpasses that of the Pharisees and the teachers of the law, you will certainly not enter the kingdom of heaven.

- *Matthew 5:17-20 NIV*

What I received from this scripture was that I was going to speak to someone who believed that they were going to heaven by keeping the law.

On the way to the airport in the shuttle my son

and I had touched and agreed that we would be on the first flight to Maui no matter what. We arrived at the airport and checked in as standby passengers.

It was crowded, the flight was oversold. There were twenty-eight standby passengers. We were, twenty-six, twenty-seven, and twenty-eight. I didn't think to tell them that we were thru passengers, it didn't cross my mind until later.

The plane was boarded and we were not called as standby passengers. We watched the plane leave the gate. When it left I said, "Ok Lord, what happened? We were supposed to be on that plane. Why weren't we on the plane?" I received no response.

We hadn't eaten yet so I suggested we go sit down and eat. While there I overheard a conversation between a man and woman. The woman was really upset. Seemed like they had been in Los Angeles, California for days and they had still not gotten on a flight.

After breakfast, on the way out of the restaurant we heard an announcement on the intercom. The agent was announcing the return of the plane that we were booked on but it was returning to a different gate. I said, "Wait a minute, didn't that plane leave?! I heard the announcement again.

I said, "Obviously not!" We ran to the gate that was announced. I approached the agent at the counter and I said, "What happened!? We were standbys on this flight. Why did it come back?" He said, "It had a mechanical problem." I said, "Lord, You know what You're doing. I'm glad I wasn't on that plane."

I then told the gate agent I said, "Listen we were listed as standby's on the flight. We are twenty-six, twenty-seven, and twenty-eight.

Obviously we didn't make it on the plane. We are thru passengers. I don't believe I mentioned that earlier, but we have been here since last night."

I then said, "I know that the flight is overbooked but if you have three seats available could you please put us on it?" He told me to stand in eyes view, where he could see me. I did exactly that.

It was a while before we left. They had to switch out planes and re-board. During the time of waiting I heard one man cancel his reservation.

After sometime they began boarding the flight again. The agent had boarded the ticketed passengers. He counted his tickets and then began boarding standby passengers.

Suddenly, he motioned for me to come. I summoned my husband and son and we approached the counter. The agent quickly gave us seat assignments and boarded us.

Finally, we were on our way to Maui! I was in awe of what Jesus had done. I was in such awe that I began thanking and praising Him down the jet way.

My husband William and I had seats together while my son sat separately from us.

When my husband and I arrived at our seats there was a lady who sat in our row. She said, "Where is the family that was sitting here before? What happened to them?" Looking at each other, William and I then looked at the lady and said, "We don't know!" The young lady then asked us, "How did you all get on the plane?" My immediate response was, "Jesus!"

She then began to ask other questions like, "Did we have a ticket?" "Did we have a reservation? And again, "How did we get on the plane? My answer again was, "Jesus!"

William began to try to explain to her about us being standby passengers. The lady wasn't comprehending what he was trying to tell her. Suddenly, I said, "Listen lady! We came all the way from Atlanta, Georgia through Dallas and

Los Angeles and now to Maui with no tickets and only two hundred dollars in our pocket.

She said, "Well, I'd like to hear how that happened?!" Again I said, "Jesus!" She replied, "Jesus can't just put you on a plane with no money." Confidently I responded, "Excuse me! Jesus can do anything He wants to do because He is God in the flesh.

He can move people, change minds. He can do anything He wants because He is God! I then added, "You've heard that it's not what you know, it's who you know. Well, we know the

God of the universe. The lady took her seat beside me. We said nothing to each other the rest of the flight.

We arrived in Maui exhausted and excited. We definitely weren't use to the time difference. It was in the afternoon when we arrived.

We had to take a shuttle to the resort. I could only pay for a one-way trip, otherwise we wouldn't be able to eat.

So, I said, "Ok Lord, Thank You for getting us back to the airport." Arriving at the resort, we were shown to our room by the manager. We settled our things in our rooms. I was so excited I began to call everyone at home to let them know we finally made it to Maui and told them what awesome things Jesus did. Everyone I spoke to was in awe of what Jesus had done.

One of my sisters told me not to worry about our needs. She said, "Ericka God wants to show out on your behalf. That regardless of what you all think you don't have. You are to walk by faith. If you all want to eat steak for dinner, then do so. In other words, don't limit Him. He is a big God so think big. No limits!"

After I finished telling her how we got to Maui she said, "You need to write a book." As soon as she said this, the Lord gave me the name for this book.

When speaking to my other sister in Christ I told her about the situation with the woman on the plane. She said, "Ericka, you were to talk to that woman about Jesus."

Thinking back to what the Lord had given me during my devotional time I said, "You know what! I was to talk to her." I had to repent because I didn't talk to the lady about Jesus. I told the Lord, "Lord, I was in such awe of what You had done that the only word that came out of my mouth was "Jesus." I forgot to tell the woman about You!"

He knew that I was in such awe of what He had done. Still, I had to repent. I sat by the woman during the entire flight and didn't talk to her about Jesus.

The sister in Christ also told me that the Lord wanted to use me while I was there, that someone needed to be saved. I told her that I was aware of this. She advised me to stay prayerful. She told me to bind distractions. I did.

We stayed in the resort that day. This day we were exhausted. Our body clocks were off. It was daytime and we wanted to go to bed.

After eating we went to bed while it was still daylight and all of us were awake at two o'clock the next morning.

A Faith Walk
DAY 3

It's our first full day here in Hawaii. I'm excited to see what the Lord has for us. During my devotion time He reminded me that this is a faith walk in Romans 4:11-12.

> [11] And he received circumcision as a sign, a seal of the righteousness that he had by faith while he was still uncircumcised. So then, he is the father of all who believe but have not been circumcised, in order that righteousness might be credited to them. [12] And he is then also the father of the circumcised who not only are circumcised but who also follow in the footsteps of the faith that our father Abraham had before he was circumcised.
>
> *-Romans 4:11-12*

He also told me to bind distractions, take communion, and stay alert spiritually. These things he confirmed through one of my sisters in Christ whom I spoke with the day before.

He has the song, "Let's Start the Party," from the *Camp Rock* movie on my heart.

I called the young man who arranged for us to get tickets to Maui to let him know of our arrival. During our conversation he said, "You know this trip cost about two thousand dollars."

This was like the second or third time he had mentioned this during the times I had spoken with him. I didn't think anything of it.

Suddenly, he then said, "You don't have the money to pay for this trip do you?" "No." I replied. "What money?" I offered the person who gave us the tickets my timeshare in exchange for the tickets."

He then said, "I told you that the person couldn't use your timeshare!" I was taken aback. "What!" I said.

"But that was the deal. I would have never agreed to take the tickets if I heard you say that the person didn't want my timeshare!

My timeshare is what the Lord told me to offer and for a person to use it to travel anywhere in the world and stay at a resort is worth more than two thousand dollars.

He then said, "Well, the person is saying that they can't use it." "The person can take the timeshare and give it to anyone he or she likes if he or she can't use it." I replied. "The person doesn't have anyone to give it to so the person wants the money," he said.

I don't have two thousand dollars." I replied. He said that this really puts him in a bad light because he was trying to help me. Now the person is saying they want their money.

I felt bad for him. I had appreciated all the trouble he went through to help us, now I've put him in a bad situation. I began to think.

It came to me that I would receive money from my schooling soon. I didn't know exactly when it would come in. So I told him about my money from school. He said that he'd let the person know of the situation.

Today we spent time getting to know the area we were in. We inquired about the activities in the area. William and I walked to the grocery store for food.

While leaving the store we spoke to some young men who were sitting outside of the store. They were in their twenties, some older. They claimed that they were homeless and that their families kicked them out of their homes. What they were really doing was hustling people out of their money. They admitted that they had assault charges and other police records. We told them about Jesus and how he has a better life for them. Their hearts were not open to receive. One young man said that he wanted to go to hell.

Returning from the store we then spent time on the beach which was across the street from our resort. Afterwards, we ate at Denny's and went to the resort to rest. Our bodies still hadn't adjusted to the time difference. We went to bed early.

A Faith Walk
DAY 4

Today I awakened with expectancy.

Wondering who it was that the Lord was

going to have me talk to and who it was He

was going to save.

I had no idea what the day held for us, but I

know the one who knows all things. I'm so

glad that He tells me things ahead of time.

As I started my day, with devotion of course,

He gave me the scripture John 11:45-57.

> [45] *Therefore many of the Jews who had come*
> *to visit Mary, and had seen what Jesus*
> *did, believed in him.* [46] *But some of them went*
> *to the Pharisees and told them what Jesus had*

done. ⁴⁷ Then the chief priests and the Pharisees called a meeting of the Sanhedrin.

"What are we accomplishing?" they asked. "Here is this man performing many signs. ⁴⁸ If we let him go on like this, everyone will believe in him, and then the Romans will come and take away both our temple and our nation."

⁴⁹ Then one of them, named Caiaphas, who was high priest that year, spoke up, "You know nothing at all! ⁵⁰ You do not realize that it is better for you that one man die for the people than that the whole nation perish."

⁵¹ He did not say this on his own, but as high priest that year he prophesied that Jesus would die for the Jewish nation, ⁵² and not only for that nation but also for the scattered children of God, to bring them together and make them one. ⁵³ So from that day on they plotted to take his life.

^{54} Therefore Jesus no longer moved about publicly among the people of Judea.Instead he withdrew to a region near the wilderness, to a village called Ephraim, where he stayed with his disciples.

^{55} When it was almost time for the Jewish Passover, many went up from the country to Jerusalem for their ceremonial cleansing before the Passover. ^{56} They kept looking for Jesus, and as they stood in the temple courts they asked one another, "What do you think? Isn't he coming to the festival at all?" ^{57} But the chief priests and the Pharisees had given orders that anyone who found out where Jesus was should report it so that they might arrest him. – John 11: 45-57 NIV

Whenever the Lord had given me theses scriptures in the past what I received was that He was reminding me that He died for everyone. This was His way of telling me that I am to tell everyone about Him not just some people.

He put the *Marine's Song* on my heart and then He spoke to my heart "Lahaina." I had not heard of this place but was sure it was a place on the island. I had to find out if it was a place on the island and how far it was from where we were.

Talk about taking me out of my comfort zone and stretching me! In the fourteen years of me serving the Lord there were a few times that

He had me address a crowd but not very often.

He has taught me how to start a conversation with strangers, ask pertinent questions, listen to where they are at and where they are coming from, and turn the conversation to talking about Him.

Now, He wanted me to go stand in the street and preach! Totally out of my comfort zone! Still, I was determined for His will to be done. I even got excited that He may save hundreds of people.

After spending my time with the Lord, walking around the condo I discovered the rules and guidelines of the place.

One of the rules were that we were to report anything that we saw needing repair to the personnel office. While I was in the restroom I saw something that I believed needed to be repaired. Directly after reading these rules and guidelines I saw the manager in the back of our condo trimming trees.

I took the opportunity to inform him of the broken item.

I went outside and approached him. He explained that what I talking about was as it should be. I also asked him about Lahaina. He told me that it was part of the island and how we could get there.

My husband, William had been speaking with the manager, so he recognized me. After telling him about the broken item. He mentioned to me that he and my husband had been having great conversations.

The manager said that he believed along the same lines as my husband. I asked him, "What do you believe?" He began to tell me what he believed about Jesus.

In doing so, he also told me about the things he had gone through and what issues he was dealing with at the present time.

Listening to him tell me his life story the Holy Spirit quickened me that he believed he was going to go to heaven by earning it. When he finished his testimony.

I informed him that one cannot be saved by trying to be a good person. His response,

"Who said I was saved!" I guess I assumed that he was saved because he spoke of being baptized in the church he attends.

Now I said the obvious thing. I asked him if he would like to accept Jesus as his personal Savior. His reply was "Yes!" so I led him to Christ.

It was awesome! Later, we met his grandchildren and I spoke to them. The Lord brought us all the way to Maui so He can save one man. I told William and Kahlil what happened. We rejoiced!

A Faith Walk
DAY 5

The Lord had saved the manager of the resort yesterday, but my work is not over.

He gave me Matthew 3:13-17 NIV.

> [13] *Then Jesus came from Galilee to the Jordan to be baptized by John.* [14] *But John tried to deter him, saying, "I need to be baptized by you, and do you come to me?"*
>
> [15] *Jesus replied, "Let it be so now; it is proper for us to do this to fulfill all righteousness." Then John consented.*
>
> [16] *As soon as Jesus was baptized, he went up out of the water. At that moment heaven was opened, and he saw the Spirit of God descending like a dove and alighting on him.* [17] *And a voice from heaven said, "This is my Son, whom I love; with him I am well pleased."*

I believe He's letting me know that He wants the manager to be baptized in water and in the Holy Spirit.

Yet, I didn't think the manager will come and ask me to be baptized. Why? Because he told me that he'd already been baptized. Into what, I don't know.

He himself said he didn't have a relationship with Jesus. So, I was going to have to approach him concerning this matter. I did. When I told him of these things and explained them to him he said he would have them done at the church he attended.

When we got up and around today it was the afternoon when we started out for Lahaina which was located in another part of the island.

Thirsty, we went to the store for water before getting on the bus. After buying water I had less than fifteen dollars in cash on me. It was six dollars for us to ride the bus all day.

Lahaina was beautiful. There were miles of shops and restaurants. The ocean was along the other side of them. We walked along the shops. There was one place that had big birds outside Tuscan birds that talked.

While walking I wanted to do as the Lord instructed. Fear came upon me. There were lots of people in this area. It was outdoors.

I allowed Kahlil to distract me. I paid more attention to what he wanted to do than what I knew the Lord told me to do.

So, we kept walking and I allowed fear to take over. I didn't preach.

Like Peter, I had allowed fear to paralyze me and keep me from walking on water. I took my eyes off Jesus and began focusing on the situation.

When Kahlil found out we had no money he wanted to go back to the condo and eat. I had put my child before Jesus. The only money we had left was what cash I had in my pocket. Which was six dollars and seventy-nine cents.

While heading back to the bus, I quickly went into prayer asking God to help, reminding Him of His promise of provision. I stayed in prayer the entire time, seeking the Lord for wisdom on how to feed my family.

While praying, I heard, "McDonald's dollar menu." So, I figured that when we got back to the mall to transfer buses we would go to the McDonald's I saw there.

We reached the Warf and the driver announced that the bus ahead of us would take us to "Kihei" the place of our destination.

For a moment I thought, "If we transfer now we won't be able to go to McDonald's. Kahlil suggested that we exit and take the bus directly because he wanted to get to the condo. There was no time to ponder the decision, so we got off and transferred buses to Kihei.

As we travelled I'm thinking, "Please forgive me Lord. I didn't do what you said and now I don't know how we're going to eat with just six dollars." I knew that there were no places where we were staying that we could all eat for this amount.

The bus to Kihei stopped by another mall. We stayed on it expecting it to take us to our resort but Kahlil noticed that the bus was turning in the opposite direction that we wanted to go. I noticed that there was a McDonald's on the corner where we were turning.

I asked the driver if we were going to Kihei, she said, "We are already in Kihei." I then asked her if she went to Kamole Beach? She replied, "No." The driver then gave us directions going in the opposite direction.

We got off the bus and began walking towards McDonalds where I was able to feed everyone. Kahlil looked to see when the next bus would be at the mall.

We had plenty of time, so we ate at McDonald's.

I'm so glad that God is faithful even when we are not and that He keeps His promises to us and doesn't give us what we deserve.

Everything had worked out for our good. He had provided. Now how He'll provide for us tomorrow was another thing. I guess we'll have to wait and see.

A Faith Walk
DAY 6

I really wanted to obey God when He told me to preach in Lahaina yesterday. I allowed my flesh to overtake me and ended up disobeying Him.

The one thing I love about Him is that He always tells me the truth. He gave me Romans 7:21-25 this morning letting me know that I had sinned against Him.

> *21 So I find this law at work: Although I want to do good, evil is right there with me.22 For in my inner being I delight in God's law; 23 but I see another law at work in me, waging war against the law of my mind and making me a prisoner of the law of sin at work within me. 24 What a wretched man I am! Who will rescue me from this body that is subject to death? 25 Thanks be*

to God, who delivers me through Jesus Christ our Lord!

So then, I myself in my mind am a slave to God's law, but in my sinful nature[a] a slave to the law of sin. –Romans7:21-2 5NIV

I believe He gave this to me because I didn't repent yesterday for disobeying Him.

I spent most of the morning seeking the Lord for provision. It came to me to call a Sister in Christ who had offered to help us if she could, if we were in a difficult situation. I hadn't spoken with her in a while.

She didn't even know we were in Hawaii.

I called her to tell her where we were and of the miracles the Lord was doing. She was glad to hear of it. She said that she would pray about helping us and get back to me.

As soon as William and Kahlil got up and around the first thing they asked me was, "What's to eat?" I had spent all morning seeking the Lord's face and received no answer from Him.

So my response was, "Why are you all asking me what's to eat! Do I look like God?! Why don't you ask Him?! Am I the only one around here who seeks the Lord?! I have been asking Him to help us and show me what to do all morning and I've received no answer from Him. So, I don't know how we are eating!" It got real quiet after this.

Everyone went their separate ways. Time went by and it was coming upon afternoon. I hadn't seen William in a while so I asked Kahlil if he had seen him. He said he had not.

I began looking for him but did not find him. I even went outside and searched. Sure enough, he was nowhere to be found.

An hour later, William came back with pizza, breadsticks and pop. I was in awe! My immediate response was, "Where did you go? And where did you get the money to buy food?

Kahlil was so hungry and excited he just jumped up and down waiting for the food to be put on the table so he could eat. William explained that he had pawned his wedding ring so we could eat. I couldn't even be angry with him. After all, we had just discussed him getting another wedding ring due to his being warped from work.

They didn't give him much for it, but it was enough for us to eat that day. Praise God!

A Faith Walk
DAY 7

A Faith Walk
DAY 7

The Lord is faithful. During my prayer time with Him this morning He gave me the story of Him feeding the five thousand in Matthew 14:13-21.

> *¹³ When Jesus heard what had happened, he withdrew by boat privately to a solitary place. Hearing of this, the crowds followed him on foot from the towns. ¹⁴ When Jesus landed and saw a large crowd, he had compassion on them and healed their sick.*

> *¹⁵ As evening approached, the disciples came to him and said, "This is a remote place, and it's already getting late. Send the crowds away, so they can go to the villages and buy themselves some food."*

> *¹⁶ Jesus replied, "They do not need to go away. You give them something to eat."*

¹⁷ "We have here only five loaves of bread and two fish," they answered.

¹⁸ "Bring them here to me," he said. ¹⁹ And he directed the people to sit down on the grass. Taking the five loaves and the two fish and looking up to heaven, he gave thanks and broke the loaves. Then he gave them to the disciples, and the disciples gave them to the people. ²⁰ They all ate and were satisfied, and the disciples picked up twelve basketfuls of broken pieces that were left over. ²¹ The number of those who ate was about five thousand men, besides women and children.

-Matthew 14:13-21 NIV

Miraculous provision! He put another sister in Christ on my heart to call. This is a sister who always gives to our ministry when she knows that the Lord is sending us out. I hadn't spoken to her in a while either so she also didn't know about our trip to Hawaii.

I called her and told her where we were and of the miraculous things the Lord was doing.

Turned out she was not in Tulsa but in Dallas. She was in need of prayer for a situation so I ministered to her.

After ministering to her she asked me if we needed money. She gave an offering of one hundred dollars toward our ministry. Turned out, there was a bank there where she could deposit the money.

After speaking with her, William and Kahlil expressed their desire to leave for home a day early so they could have some time to rest. I knew in my Spirit that we were not to leave but I followed.

I prepared everything to leave. I called the young man who arranged for us to get tickets and asked him to make reservations for us to return home.

Then I asked the manager of the resort if he could take us to the airport. We were checking out a day early. He was glad to take us. His wife came along. So, we were able to meet her too. Also, being hungry before we left we were able to go to Subway.

We arrived at the airport. Went to the gate to check in, only to encounter a very rude agent who told me that we were not going to get on the flight. I asked if she would put us on the standby list anyway. We waited.

The flight left without us. Not wanting to wait around, we decided to take our original flight the next day. I reluctantly called the manager at the resort and asked if he could come get us and take us back to the resort. Turned out, he

was glad to help. He even gave us the same

resort room and said he would take us to the

airport tomorrow.

A Faith Walk
DAY 8

We woke early and went to eat at Moose McGuillicuties. The manager was not at the office when we checked out. We were told he would be back in the office soon.

After breakfast we took more pictures and walked back to the resort. The manager was at the office and we waited for him to take us to the airport.

Arriving at the airport around noon our flight didn't leave until 4:10pm. The time went by quickly and they began to board the flight. Turned out, the same gate agents who worked the night before were working this flight again today.

I went to the gate to check in and the same agent told me that I was not going to make this flight either. She said that I should come back tomorrow. I could tell that this young lady didn't like me.

We sat and waited to be called to board the flight. Kahlil and I agreed and prayed that we would get on this flight. We weren't called.

After the plane boarded I went back to the gate counter to ask to be rolled over to the next flight and rebooked through Atlanta. It seemed that our only option was to get on a flight to Los Angeles which was also booked.

There were also other standby passengers trying to get on this flight. I asked the agent if she could check to see what our chances were for getting on the flight to Los Angeles. She didn't answer me.

Trying to make a decision I called the young man who was helping us with the tickets to see if he could look up the status of the flights and give me a better idea of how things looked. He suggested we go through Los Angeles.

So, I told the agent that we'd go through Los Angeles. She transferred us to the Los Angeles flight which was overbooked and delayed until ten forty-five in the evening. She did this but she didn't book us all the way through to Atlanta.

I was concerned about this so I again called the young man. He told me that the agent should have booked us through to Atlanta and given us a boarding pass for the next flight. I asked if he could do this. He said he couldn't.

He advised me to go to the ticket counter and tell them what happened. So, I did.

I left the gate area and security to go see an agent at the ticket counter. I arrived at the ticket counter and told the agent the situation. He went into a back room. When he came out he said, "Didn't the gate agent already tell you that she couldn't book you through to Atlanta until you get on this flight?"

I asked him, "Why is that when they've done it before?" He then said that his supervisor told him that he couldn't do what I was asking him.

I walked away from the counter angry. The Holy Spirit quickly reminded me that I was not wrestling against flesh and blood, but rulers, powers, and principalities in high places. It came to me! Satan was trying to keep us from getting home.

Realizing this, I went to battle in the Spirit. I declared we were going to get on this next flight to Los Angeles. I asked the Lord to remove the gate agent that was working this flight if she didn't want to cooperate with His plan.

I stayed in prayer as I made my way back through security and to the gate again. I began praying for the agent and I continually prayed through the night on and off.

It was now seven o'clock in the evening. We hadn't eaten since breakfast and we were hungry. We went to Burger King to eat. I prayed that I had enough money to pay for food. Turned out that I did have the money. After dinner we went back to the gate.

Nothing to do but hurry up and wait. More people came to the gate and we soon found out that the flight would not arrive until 12:50a.m. and depart at one-thirty in the morning.

After a while some people left and others rebooked flights for another time. We had to stay regardless. I was just praying that the flight didn't cancel.

Kahlil and William both dosed off. For some reason I was not able to sleep. I was wide awake, praying. I ended up talking to a passenger who said he was a bible teacher at his church. I testified about the miracles God was doing and had done on this trip. He was amazed.

Still waiting, I couldn't sit any longer, so I decided to walk the terminal. I walked where there were no people and no flights being boarded so that I could be alone and hear the Lord. In doing this, the Lord but the song, "Na, Na, Na, Na Goodbye," on my heart. Not long after hearing this from the Lord I felt an urgency to go back to the gate.

As I was returning to the gate there was an announcement made by one of the airlines.

I asked a person who made the announcement? She said, "United just cancelled their flight to Los Angeles."

Immediately, I thought, "No! Now they will book their people on our flight and the plane will be full." Back at the gate, the Lord still has the "Goodbye" song on my heart. The gate agents have arrived at the gate and began giving out blankets to passengers and inquiring about their connecting flights. They are also preparing for the arrival of the plane.

A group of United passengers walked by the gate and asked where our flight was going. The agent told the man our destination. He hollers to the others who were quickly walking away to inform them of this information but they didn't stop.

Nevertheless, there were some people from other airlines who transferred to our flight. Still, the Lord was reassuring me that we would make it on this plane.

A Faith Walk
DAY 9

Still awaiting the planes arrival. William brought to my attention to a lady that was standing in line to check in at the gate.

It turned out that it was the same lady that we sat by on the plane to Maui. The lady that I was supposed to speak to about Jesus.

As I sat there looking at her I realized what the Lord had done. He made it that we couldn't leave Friday like we wanted and that we miss the first flight yesterday to give me another chance to witness to this lady about Him. This time I was going to be obedient.

William got her attention as I walked over to her as she was in line. She recognized us and was glad to see us.

She said, "What a coincidence that we are on the same flight going home." I told her our situation. That we had tried to leave Friday and yesterday but wasn't able to do so. I then said, "Now I understand why things happened as they did." She asked me, "Why?"

I said, "You know on the plane in Los Angeles on the way here when you were asking us questions about how we got on the plane and all I could say was, "Jesus." "Yes." She replied. "Well, I would like to tell you about Jesus."

She said something about being religious and I told her that I wasn't religious and Jesus is not about a religion but it's a personal relationship with the "Creator" of the universe.

She then told me that she was Jewish and that this day was the day her people celebrated the Holy day of Yon Kippur, the Day of Atonement.

I thought to myself, "That's great because I'd like to tell you about how Jesus is the atonement for our sins."

I began to tell her about Jesus and what He had done for her. She then told me how her brother had converted from Judaism to Christianity and he's always trying to tell her about Jesus.

Then she politely changed the subject by saying that she was extremely tired. Her way of telling me that she didn't want to discuss the subject.

I didn't push the subject because I know that she probably was tired like everyone else from waiting on the plane all night. Plus, Jesus doesn't push himself on anyone.

 I changed the subject. She then began to complain about the service of the airlines. Others heard her and joined in. It was now time for me to step out of the picture so I sat down.

Shortly after, the plane arrived. Everyone was checked in but we now had to wait for the plane to be serviced. I also noticed that the agent who I prayed to be removed was not the gate agent for this flight.

Finally, we boarded the plane. William and I had first class seats so we were among those who boarded first. We were comfortably seated in the first row when the lady I was speaking to boarded with the rest of the passengers and saw us seated in first class.

Again, she looked at us in amazement and wonder as to say, "How did they get first class?" She now understood what we meant by standby.

What she said was, "You all are so lucky!"

"No, we're blessed," said William. Then I replied, "There's no such thing as luck!"

We arrived in Los Angeles around ten-thirty in the morning and went directly to check in for the next flight. It's normal for flights out of Los Angeles to Dallas to be overbooked and this one was no exception.

 We didn't make the first two flights. The next one was at three o'clock in the afternoon. Inquiring about connections I was informed that if we didn't make the three o'clock afternoon flight that we would miss the last connection to Atlanta.

While waiting to see if we would be seated on the three o'clock plane, William and I engaged in conversation with a woman who was also a standby passenger.

We told her of our journey to Maui and how God is miraculously providing for our trip. She shared some things about her life and God. She asked for prayer for herself and her family and told us she wanted to give us some money toward our ministry for food.

We prayed and decided to meet each other at the gate.

William, Kahlil, and myself hadn't eaten all day so we went to get something to eat. The woman had given us twenty dollars for food. It was on time. It turned out that I didn't have enough money on my card to pay for what we were buying to eat.

God knew this, that's why He had her give us the money. After purchasing the food, we proceeded to the gate and waited to see if we would make the three o'clock afternoon flight.

While praying, we asked that we would all have a seat on the plane. The woman who was also a standby passenger had a higher priority ticket than ours.

We knew that she would be called to board before us. It seemed as though they had a larger plane for this flight. The plane was being boarded.

The woman was boarded before us. As she was boarding she said, "I'm sorry you all didn't make it." I replied, "We prayed that we all make it. They are not finished boarding yet." As it was, we were the last ones to board the plane, but we made it.

The plane was full, so they made us check our bags. The bags were only checked to Dallas because the agent didn't have time to check our connecting flight to Atlanta. But, I didn't find this out until we arrived in Dallas.

On the plane we were separated. I sat between a Hispanic woman and a man. William and Kahlil sat in the back of the plane together. As soon as I sat down I engaged in a conversation with the man I was sitting next to. I said, "Do you know that my family and I travelled all the way from Atlanta to Maui with no tickets and less than two hundred dollars in our pocket?"

He said, "How did you do that?" Thus began me telling him of the miraculous things God was doing on our trip. He was amazed.

 I then asked him if Jesus was his personal Savior? He declared that He was. As I began to ask him more indebt questions he began to change the subject so I quit asking.

A Faith Walk
DAY 10

We arrived in Dallas at 8:15p.m. By the time we got off the plane it was close to 8:30p.m.

Our plane to Atlanta was to depart at 9:30p.m. I departed the plane before William and Kahlil so I asked the gate agent if she would list us as standby passengers for the Atlanta flight.

When William and Kahlil got off the plane I was informed that both of our bags were checked to Dallas and not to Atlanta. Knowing from experience how baggage claim is I decided that we would retrieve our bags from baggage claim before going to the gate.

The agent interjected and said that we would miss our flight if we retrieved our bags. That our gate was in Concourse C and we were in Concourse A. Baggage claim was also in Concourse A.

Almost believing her we proceeded to Concourse C. My spirit was not settled with leaving our bags and filing a claim in Atlanta.

So, I decided to retrieve our bags. I sent William and Kahlil to the gate with all the tickets and I proceeded to run to the baggage claim area. I ran through most of the airport stopping to catch my breath periodically.

When I arrived at baggage claim the luggage was already loaded off from our flight and going around the turnstile. I grabbed our bags as soon as I saw them. I then began running towards security.

I reached security only to realize that I didn't have my ticket and therefore I couldn't proceed. The security agent sent me to the ticket counter where there was a line.

In a hurry, I tried to check myself in but couldn't so I finally stood in line. There were only three people ahead of me but it seemed as though they were taking a long time.

Finally, my turn at the counter. I proceeded to explain my situation to the agent. She gave me a boarding pass, looked at the time it was close to 9:00p.m.

I proceeded to security only to find the line backed up and only one security line open. I became frustrated and impatient as I stripped myself of my shoes and jacket.

I couldn't rush security. Making it through security I hurriedly put on my shoes and gathered my belongings.

Wanting to run to the gate my first thought after looking at the time was that I would never make it. I had to make it to the Skyline to catch it to Concourse C. It was past 9:00p.m. and I knew they had begun boarding the plane.

As plain as day I heard the Holy Spirit say to me, "You haven't given up in all this time, why would you give up now?" I immediately began running. I also thought, "If anyone wants to find out if they are in shape or not they need to try this."

I had to make it to the Skyline to get to Concourse C and I had less than fifteen minutes to make it.

I reached the Skyline. Seemed as though it took forever for it to come. It made one stop before reaching Concourse C.

Arriving in Concourse C, I again began running toward the escalator to reach gate C 2.

I reached the top of the escalator and there Kahlil was waiting for me at the bottom. I got off the escalator, gave him a bag and told him to run ahead to the gate.

I continued running behind him. I could see William at the gate. I heard him yell to the agents, "Here she comes!" Everyone had boarded the plane. They were holding it for me.

As I arrived at the gate the agents began to applaud saying, "You made it!" We hurried on the plane and took our seats.

We were all seated together on this flight. I took time to write in my journal. William read. And, Kahlil went to sleep.

The Lord put the reggae song with the words, *"Don't worry about a thing. Every little thing is going to be alright,"* on my heart. He kept this song on my heart even when we arrived in Atlanta.

I believed it had something to do with parking. We didn't have the money to pay for parking. So, the Lord was telling me ahead of time not to worry about it. We arrived in

Atlanta, proceeded to the garage, found our car, and proceeded to pay for parking. What happened was what I expected.

I tried using my debit card but it came back "insufficient funds." I tried several times with the same result. The last time the machine took my ticket.

Knowing that I didn't have the money I was hesitant to go to the cashier. I got the cashier's attention to inform her that the machine took my ticket.

She called the manager to retrieve it for me. We sat there at least ten minutes waiting for the manager who retrieved the ticket and gave it back to us. I then tried it again.

I tried every debit card I had knowing that we had nothing on them. I prayed the entire time for wisdom on what to do.

It was inevitable. I had to change lanes and go to the cashier's lane. Still acting as though I had money on my debit cards, I proceeded to run them through as if it wasn't going to say, "insufficient funds."

As I was doing this I heard the cashier on the phone speaking to someone. She said, "I don't know what this lady is doing? She doesn't have any money."

When she got off the phone she said, "Lady, you don't have any money do you?" I admitted that I didn't. She then proceeded to call the manager as we waited.

While waiting for the manager cars began to pile up behind me. Now I was embarrassed. The cashier then told me to park over to the side and wait for him.

While waiting I continued to pray. I prayed that we would have favor with the manager. When the manager showed up he gave us a sheet of paper with options of how to pay the fee.

He informed us that we could have someone fax their credit card information to him. I said, "How are we going to find someone who would do this at one o'clock in the morning?"

I then explained that we were new to the area and didn't really know anyone. He asked if we lived in Atlanta.

I said, "No, we live in Trion, Georgia. The man had no mercy. It was like, "Pay the fee this way or you'll be here."

He soon left. William got out of the car and began walking around. I kept praying in the Spirit. Then it came to me to see if I could get ahold of our bank and see if some money I was expecting had come through my account.

I called. It turned out that the money wasn't going to post until later. The agent on the phone asked me if I needed any other assistance. I began thinking.

Suddenly, I asked her about overdraft protection. I knew I didn't have it.

The agent began to explain the process to me and how it applied to my debit card. I asked the agent if I could receive overdraft protection while we were speaking. The agent said, "Yes." She told me that it was done immediately and that it was available for my use.

I hung up the phone and told William and Kahlil about it. We prayed one last time about using the card. After praying, the Lord said,

"It shall be done."

I drove to the cashier, told her that I was going to try my card one last time. I put in my ticket and entered my card. It was approved.

Praise God!!! We were now on our way home. We arrived home at four-thirty Monday morning.

It's Not Over

Til It's Over

Home at last! Hawaii was wonderful. God did amazing things. I continued to testify of His wonderful works to everyone I spoke with.

It took days for our bodies to adjust to the time difference. Yet, even though we were home the battle continued.

What battle? The entire trip was a spiritual battle as well as a physical one. It wasn't over,

I still had unfinished business with the young man who arranged for our travel. I had told him that I would give him the money for our trip when my school funds arrived. I had every intention of doing this. Every day I prayed and asked the Lord for the money to give to this young man for our travel.

Whenever I would ask the Lord this question there was an uneasiness in my Spirit. I began to go over the events that happened in my mind. What the Lord had told me.

Coming to the same conclusion every time. That He had told me to offer my time-share.

Confusion had set in. As I spoke with the young man, I was still trying to find a way for the time-share to be used. I told him that I could give it to him and he could give it to anyone he wanted. He said that He couldn't use it either. I asked him if he knew of anyone who could use it and I would sell it to them.

He'd said He'd try. In the end, he said he could find no one who wanted it.

Daily, I took this concern to the Lord. I would say, "Lord You said that You would pay for our trip so tell me what to do?"

Then it came to me. If the Lord sent us on the trip then it's for Him to pay for it, not me."

Even though I would come to this conclusion every time, I still felt obligated to find a way to pay this young man back.

Confusion!

One day while speaking to one of my sisters in Christ about the details of our return home from Hawaii I also mentioned the situation I was in.

Immediately, she gave me insight into the situation. First she asked me, "Did God tell you to give the young man money to pay for your tickets? "No", I replied.

He told me to offer my time-share to whoever gave us the tickets." "Then why are you trying to give this man money?" She replied. I told her that the young man said that the person who gave us the tickets claimed she didn't want the time-share.

That she couldn't use it. I told him that she could give it to someone else. I even offered it to him, but he claimed he couldn't use it either.

She then informed me that Satan was trying to steal my testimony. How? I had already defeated Satan. I was testifying about what Jesus had done on the way to Hawaii, in Hawaii, on the way home, and now even when I returned home. True, even so, Satan was trying to steal my testimony.

She reminded me that in my testimony I am telling others that we went to Hawaii without paying for plane tickets. This was true.

So, if Satan can get me to give this young man money for the travel we took then it would look like we paid our own way to Hawaii, not

God. This would steal the glory from God and make my testimony void.

Now the light was on! The reason I felt uneasy in my Spirit whenever I thought about paying this young man back was because I wasn't to pay him. I should have never told him that I would give him any money.

Now, I had to repent and also apologize to him for telling him that I could pay him. This was not going to be easy. I knew he would be very upset. The woman who gave us the tickets was pressuring him for the money.

Now I had to tell him that I would not be giving him any money for the tickets and ask for his forgiveness.

It would make me look bad, as if I were lying. At this moment I had to choose whether I wanted to hold on to my reputation or glorify God.

It didn't take me long to decide that I wanted God to be glorified and that Satan was not going to steal my testimony.

My sister asked me if I wanted her to be on the other line while I spoke with the young man to help him understand. I refused her offer

knowing that this was something I had to do

on my own.

Taking a deep breath, after I finished speaking

with my sister. I called the young man.

I informed him that I would not be giving him

money for the plane tickets. I explained that

the only thing I could give him or the lady

who gave us the tickets was my time-share. I

then told him that I should have never offered

him money because it was not what God told

me to do. I apologized and asked for his forgiveness.

As expected, he was very angry. He said some harsh things to me. Including that he thought I was taking advantage of him and never intended to pay for the trip we took.

Again, I informed him that I had offered my time-share and to my knowledge that was accepted. I informed him that my time-share was worth more than the trip we took and that the offer was still on the table if he or the lady wanted it.

He continued to speak angrily toward me. In order to keep my composure, I took the phone from my ear. Finally, I just hung up.

One would think, "Well, I've done the hard part, it is over. That's not how Satan works. He doesn't give up.

After I hung up he tried to make me feel guilty as if I was the one who had done something wrong. The only thing I had done wrong was to offer the young man money God didn't tell me to offer. I had repented for this. I knew I was forgiven.

The accuser had no right to accuse me of

anything but that didn't stop him from trying.

I didn't allow him to put a guilt trip on me.

Now it is over! Satan has not stolen my

testimony and God is being glorified!

I believe the Lord wanted me to write this book to encourage the Body of Christ. As believers we are to live and walk by faith daily.

"For we live by faith, not by sight."
– 2 Corinthians 5:7 NIV

"Clearly no one who relies on the law is justified before God, because "the righteous will live by faith."
– Galatians 3:11 NIV

As the Lord said to me several times during this journey. "This is a faith walk!"

Meaning, that every day and every hour of the day we are to put on our armor, get instructions from our Commander and Chief, and follow His lead. Doing this will call for us to do some things that are not considered "normal" as the world sees it.

As the "Church," we are not called to lead a hum-drum life. We are called to live an extraordinary life. We cannot live by faith and put God in a box. He is limitless. According to Isaiah 55:8, *"For my thoughts are not your thoughts, neither are your ways my ways," declares the Lord."*

He has delivered us to live a life of freedom in Him, but we must trust Him.

Have you heard the saying, "Watch what you say, it just might happen?" Well, as you can see I heard someone's testimony, opened my mouth and God made it happen.

He let me see for myself the level of my faith. It is His desire for us to grow in faith and trust in our Lord.

As you can see, at the beginning I didn't think I had the level of faith that the young lady had. I desired it, but I didn't know if I could do what she did. I didn't know, but God did. He allowed me to see for myself where my faith was.

No, I didn't do everything perfectly and He was trying to stretch my faith and take me out of my comfort zone. I failed at this at some point. Even still, He was there to catch me. He remained faithful to me even when I wasn't faithful to Him.

What I learned on this journey was invaluable. Some things I already knew from walking with the Lord for many years like: Stay in prayer

1. Acknowledge the Lord in all my ways

2. Be quick to repent of sin

3. Keep my armor on

4. Listen and obey the Lord

5. Being in the Lord's "will" doesn't mean you won't have trouble or go through anything. It's just the opposite.

I learned to trust the Lord more, that I really didn't know the meaning of the scripture, "*My grace is sufficient,*" and I learned how to apply the concept of binding and losing to my life.

So you see, because of Jesus I really am a conqueror and so are you!

How do I know?

Because the Word of God says, *"They triumphed over him by the blood of the Lamb and by the word of their testimony;"* Revelation 12:11a NIV

The devil was defeated from the start of this trip because I testified about Jesus and His miraculous works the entire time.

Don't ever let the devil steal your testimony. Your testimony glorifies what God has done in your life and it can save someone else's life.

You too can walk on water daily.

How?

By believing what God has told you to do and applying it to your life, keeping your eyes on Jesus and not your circumstances, daily putting on your armor, staying in prayer and praise, acknowledging Him in all your ways, listening and obeying His voice, being quick to repent of sin when you miss it, and Never! Ever! Give up!

Hi! I'm Ericka Wilson. I was born and raised in Chicago, Illinois. I have raised two amazing sons who both serve the Lord Jesus Christ. They are married to two gorgeous and awesome women. My sons are fifteen years apart and I have three off the chain gorgeous granddaughters and one great grandson.

I claim no accolades. I have no Ph.D. except in Jesus. I can only say that I am who my Father God says I am.

He has called me to be a light to this world. I am an

Ambassador for the Kingdom of God. He has

anointed me and appointed me to be an

Apostle/Prophet to the body of Christ.

Coming Soon!

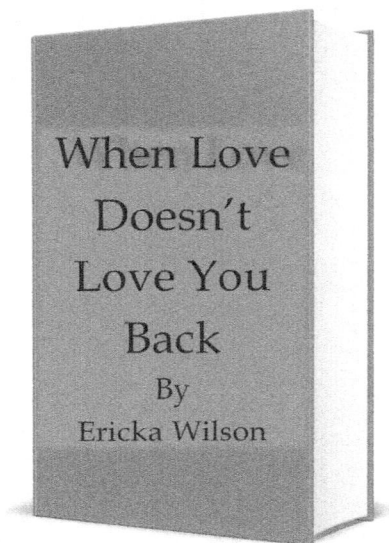

When Love
Doesn't
Love You
Back
By
Ericka Wilson

Do You Have a Book that Needs to Published?

Are You an Inspiring Author?

Sign Up Today
for the
I WRITE IT NOW (IWIN)
Self-Publishing Course

A 5-week self-publishing course that helps authors write and publish their book.

Register Now
at
www.IWRITEITNOW.com

Iwin@writenow.global

AC Creative™
Set Apart. From the Start

Made in the USA
Monee, IL
10 October 2021